Pisces Horoscope 2025

By

Thalia C. Astraea

Table of Contents
Pisces (Feb. 19 – Mar. 20)

Personality

Pisces (February 19 – March 20), symbolized by the Fish, is a Water sign ruled by Neptune. Known for their intuition, creativity, and compassionate nature, Pisces individuals are deeply connected to their emotions and the world around them. They possess a unique ability to empathize with others and often have an artistic or spiritual outlook on life.

Core Traits of Pisces

1. **Empathetic and Compassionate:** Pisces are natural empaths, deeply attuned to the emotions and needs of others. They often prioritize helping those around them.
2. **Creative and Imaginative:** Their rich inner world fuels a talent for artistic expression, whether through art, music, writing, or other forms of creativity.
3. **Intuitive and Mystical:** Guided by their intuition, Pisces often have an almost psychic ability to sense what's beneath the surface.
4. **Adaptable and Open-Minded:** Like water, Pisces can flow with the circumstances around them, making them flexible and accepting of change.

5. **Romantic and Dreamy:** Pisces are deeply idealistic and often dream of a better world, which influences their relationships and life goals.

Strengths of Pisces

- **Compassion:** Pisces is incredibly understanding and always willing to lend a listening ear or a helping hand.
- **Creativity:** Their imaginative mind allows them to excel in artistic and innovative pursuits.
- **Intuition:** Pisces have a strong inner compass that helps them make decisions and connect with others on a deeper level.
- **Flexibility:** They adapt easily to different situations and are willing to explore new ideas and experiences.
- **Altruism:** Pisces are selfless and often put the needs of others before their own, driven by a desire to make the world a better place.

Weaknesses of Pisces

- **Overly Sensitive:** Pisces can take criticism or negativity to heart, which may lead to self-doubt or withdrawal.
- **Escapism:** They may retreat into their dreams or distractions when faced with stress or overwhelming emotions.

- **Indecisiveness:** Their tendency to see all sides of a situation can make decision-making difficult.
- **Overgiving:** Pisces may neglect their own needs while focusing on others, leading to burnout or emotional exhaustion.
- **Easily Influenced:** Their open-hearted nature may leave them vulnerable to manipulation or taking on others' emotions.

Pisces in Relationships

As Partners:

Pisces are deeply romantic and value emotional intimacy in relationships. They are attentive, caring, and willing to go above and beyond for their loved ones.

- **Strengths in Love:** Loyal, affectionate, and intuitive, Pisces brings warmth and depth to their relationships.
- **Challenges in Love:** Their idealism may lead to unrealistic expectations, and their emotional sensitivity may cause conflicts if not addressed with understanding.

As Friends:

Pisces are supportive and dependable friends who provide a safe space for others to express their feelings.

Their kindness and empathy make them highly valued in any social circle.

- **Strengths in Friendship:** Loyal, understanding, and always ready to help.
- **Challenges in Friendship:** Their tendency to avoid confrontation may lead to unresolved issues.

As Family Members:

Pisces are devoted and nurturing family members, often taking on the role of the emotional anchor in their households.

Pisces in Career and Professional Life

Pisces thrive in careers that allow them to express their creativity or help others. Their intuitive nature and adaptability make them valuable in various professional settings.

Ideal Career Paths:

- **Creative Arts:** Pisces excels in fields like writing, music, film, and visual arts due to their vivid imagination and emotional depth.
- **Healthcare or Therapy:** Their compassion and empathy suit roles like counseling, nursing, or social work.

- **Spiritual or Mystical Fields:** Pisces often find fulfillment in careers involving spirituality, astrology, or holistic healing.
- **Humanitarian Work:** They are naturally drawn to roles where they can make a positive impact on others' lives.
- **Education or Mentorship:** Their patience and ability to inspire others make them great teachers or mentors.

Workplace Traits:

- **Strengths:** Pisces bring creativity, teamwork, and intuition to their work.
- **Challenges:** They may struggle with practical details or become overwhelmed in high-pressure environments.

Pisces and Personal Growth

To reach their full potential, Pisces can benefit from developing stronger boundaries and focusing on self-care.

Tips for Personal Growth:

1. **Set Boundaries:** Learn to say no and prioritize your well-being.

2. **Embrace Practicality:** Balance your dreams with actionable steps to achieve them.
3. **Develop Resilience:** Build emotional strength to navigate criticism and challenges.
4. **Focus on Self-Care:** Take time to recharge and reflect without overcommitting to others' needs.
5. **Be Decisive:** Trust your intuition to make confident choices without overthinking.

Pisces Compatibility

- **Best Matches:** Taurus, Cancer, Scorpio, and Capricorn—these signs appreciate Pisces' emotional depth, creativity, and sensitivity.
- **Challenging Matches:** Gemini and Sagittarius, whose practicality and adventurous nature may clash with Pisces' dreamy and emotional tendencies.

Conclusion

Pisces are compassionate, intuitive, and creative individuals who excel at connecting with others on a deep emotional level. While their sensitivity and selflessness are among their greatest strengths, focusing on self-care, setting boundaries, and embracing practicality will help them achieve their dreams and maintain balance. Pisces' unique ability to blend imagination with empathy allows them to bring beauty, inspiration, and healing to the world around them.

Introduce

Pisces (February 19 – March 20), 2025 will be a year of profound growth, emotional exploration, and creative breakthroughs. With your natural intuition and adaptability, you'll navigate the year's opportunities and challenges with grace. The planetary alignments in 2025 encourage you to embrace your dreams while remaining grounded in reality, allowing you to bring your imaginative ideas to life in a tangible way.

As a deeply compassionate and spiritual sign, you'll find yourself drawn to meaningful connections and transformative experiences throughout the year. From career advancements to emotional growth, Pisces will experience a blend of introspection and dynamic action. This year will challenge you to balance your idealistic nature with practical steps, creating a foundation for long-term success and fulfillment.

Overall Energy for Pisces in 2025

The year begins with Saturn in your sign, bringing a sense of discipline and focus. While Saturn's energy may feel heavy at times, it encourages you to take responsibility for your goals and lay the groundwork for your future. This transit is an excellent time to reassess your priorities and commit to personal growth.

Jupiter, your traditional ruler, spends the first half of the year in Taurus, supporting financial growth, intellectual pursuits, and stability. This placement encourages you to explore new opportunities in learning, communication, and networking. In the second half of the year, Jupiter moves into Gemini, shifting your focus to adaptability, collaboration, and exploring innovative ideas.

Neptune, your modern ruler, remains in your sign, amplifying your creativity, intuition, and spiritual growth. However, Neptune's influence also reminds you to stay grounded and avoid escapism. Pluto's brief return to Aquarius highlights introspection and the opportunity to release old patterns, paving the way for a more authentic version of yourself.

Career and Ambition

2025 is a transformative year for Pisces in terms of career and professional growth. Saturn in your sign encourages a disciplined and structured approach to your goals. While this may feel challenging, it provides the clarity and determination needed to build a solid foundation for long-term success.

Jupiter in Taurus supports creative projects, networking, and intellectual pursuits in the first half of the year. This is an excellent time to expand your skills, explore new career opportunities, or work on projects that align with your values. In the second half of the year, Jupiter's shift into Gemini inspires dynamic collaboration, adaptability, and innovation in your professional life.

- **Key Opportunities:** Promotions, creative ventures, and networking will shine in 2025.
- **Challenges:** Balancing your idealism with the practical steps needed to achieve your goals.

Tips for Career Success in 2025:

1. Embrace Saturn's discipline to stay focused and organized.
2. Use Jupiter's expansive energy to explore opportunities for growth and collaboration.
3. Stay adaptable and open to new ideas, especially during the latter half of the year.

Finance and Wealth

Financially, 2025 offers stability and opportunities for growth. Jupiter in Taurus emphasizes practicality, encouraging you to focus on saving, budgeting, and building financial security. This is a great time to reassess your financial goals and make thoughtful investments in areas that align with your values.

In the second half of the year, Jupiter's shift to Gemini may bring unexpected opportunities to diversify your income or collaborate on new ventures. However, it's essential to remain cautious and avoid impulsive financial decisions.

- **Key Opportunities:** Steady income growth, creative investments, and financial stability.
- **Challenges:** Avoiding overspending on indulgences or distractions.

Tips for Financial Success in 2025:

1. Create a practical budget and stick to it.
2. Seek advice before making significant financial decisions or investments.
3. Focus on long-term goals rather than short-term gratification.

Love and Relationships

Relationships take on greater depth and significance for Pisces in 2025. With Saturn in your sign, you're encouraged to set boundaries, communicate clearly, and build connections based on mutual trust and respect. This is a year to deepen existing relationships and attract meaningful new ones.

For singles, the first half of the year brings opportunities to meet someone special through intellectual pursuits, social events, or creative activities. Emotional compatibility and shared values will play a key role in forming lasting connections.

For those in relationships, this is a year to strengthen emotional intimacy, resolve conflicts, and align your future goals with your partner. Jupiter's influence in Gemini later in the year encourages open communication and shared adventures.

- **For Singles:** Reflect on your relationship goals and take your time building meaningful connections.
- **For Those in Relationships:** Focus on trust, communication, and creating shared experiences.

Challenges in Love:

- Managing emotional sensitivity and avoiding overidealizing partners.
- Balancing your need for personal space with nurturing your relationships.

Tips for Love and Relationships in 2025:

1. Be open and honest about your feelings and expectations.
2. Practice active listening and empathy to strengthen connections.
3. Celebrate small moments of joy and appreciation in your relationships.

Health and Wellness

Health is a priority for Pisces in 2025, with Saturn encouraging you to focus on self-discipline and balance. This is a year to establish sustainable wellness routines that support both physical and mental well-being.

The first half of the year is ideal for grounding practices like yoga, mindfulness, or spending time in nature. As the pace picks up in the latter half of the year, prioritize relaxation and self-care to avoid burnout.

- **Physical Health:** Focus on building strength and resilience through regular exercise and healthy eating.
- **Mental and Emotional Health:** Embrace reflective practices like journaling or meditation to manage stress and gain clarity.

Challenges in Health:

- Overworking or neglecting rest during busy periods.
- Managing stress or emotional tension caused by responsibilities.

Tips for Health and Wellness in 2025:

1. Create a balanced routine that includes exercise, relaxation, and mindfulness.
2. Listen to your body's signals and avoid pushing yourself too hard.
3. Dedicate time to hobbies or creative outlets that bring joy and relaxation.

Personal Growth and Spirituality

2025 is a year of profound personal growth and transformation for Pisces. Neptune's influence in your sign enhances your spiritual connection, creativity, and intuition. Saturn encourages you to integrate these insights into your daily life, creating a balanced and purposeful approach to your growth.

Pluto's brief return to Aquarius offers a chance to release old patterns and embrace a more authentic version of yourself. This is a year to explore your spiritual beliefs, connect with like-minded individuals, and align your actions with your inner values.

Key Themes:

- Emotional growth, self-reflection, and building resilience.
- Exploring creativity, spirituality, and personal purpose.

Tips for Personal Growth in 2025:

1. Trust your intuition to guide you toward meaningful opportunities.
2. Surround yourself with supportive and inspiring people.
3. Celebrate your progress and embrace change with courage.

Conclusion

2025 is a year of transformation, creativity, and emotional depth for Pisces. By balancing your dreams with practical steps, focusing on meaningful connections, and prioritizing self-care, you'll navigate the year with confidence and clarity. This is a time to embrace your unique gifts, trust your intuition, and build a future that reflects your highest aspirations.

January

January 2025 is a month of focus, reflection, and progress for Pisces. With Saturn in your sign, you're encouraged to approach your goals with discipline and determination. The energy of the Capricorn and Aquarius seasons supports grounding, innovation, and building meaningful connections. This is a powerful time to reassess your priorities, establish a strong foundation, and set the tone for the year ahead.

Work

January emphasizes focus and planning in Pisces' professional life.

- **Opportunities:** Saturn's influence encourages long-term planning and disciplined action. This is a great time to tackle complex projects, take on responsibilities, and showcase your creativity. Networking with colleagues may lead to valuable opportunities.
- **Challenges:** Avoid overanalyzing or becoming overwhelmed by responsibilities. Maintain patience with slower processes.

Advice: Focus on organization and consistency. Break larger goals into manageable steps to avoid feeling overwhelmed.

Finance

Your financial outlook in January highlights stability and cautious growth.

- **Opportunities:** This is a favorable time to review your budget, prioritize savings, and explore opportunities for additional income. Investments in practical ventures may yield steady returns.
- **Challenges:** Avoid impulsive spending, particularly on items that may not align with your long-term goals.

Advice: Stick to a disciplined budget and focus on aligning financial decisions with your priorities.

Love

January brings warmth and introspection to Pisces' love life.

- **For Singles:** Take time to reflect on what you truly want in a partner. Opportunities for meaningful connections may arise through mutual friends, creative activities, or work.
- **For Those in Relationships:** Focus on open communication and creating stability with your partner. Thoughtful gestures and shared experiences will help deepen your bond.

Advice: Be authentic and patient in your interactions. Use this time to nurture trust and emotional intimacy.

Health

Health-wise, January encourages Pisces to prioritize balance and self-care.

- **Strengths:** Saturn's influence supports establishing consistent wellness routines that enhance both physical and mental well-being.
- **Challenges:** Overworking or neglecting rest may lead to fatigue if not managed properly.

Advice: Incorporate mindfulness practices like meditation or yoga into your routine. Focus on maintaining a balanced diet, staying hydrated, and getting adequate sleep.

Be Careful

- **Overworking:** Avoid taking on too many responsibilities, as this could lead to stress or burnout.
- **Neglecting Self-Care:** Balance your ambition with relaxation to maintain overall well-being.
- **Emotional Sensitivity:** Practice mindfulness to manage emotions and avoid overreacting to minor conflicts.

<u>*Advice*</u>

1. **Plan Strategically:** Use Saturn's disciplined energy to set clear and realistic goals for the year.
2. **Nurture Relationships:** Focus on building trust and emotional depth in your connections.
3. **Practice Balance:** Prioritize self-care and relaxation alongside your ambitions.

<u>*Additional Tips*</u>

- **Lucky Days:** January 9, 16, and 25 – Ideal for decision-making, creative pursuits, or building relationships.
- **Lucky Color:** Sea Green – This color symbolizes balance, renewal, and harmony.
- **Affirmation for January:** *"I align my actions with my purpose, creating stability and growth in all areas of my life."*

January 2025 is a month of focus and preparation for Pisces. By concentrating on meaningful goals, disciplined planning, and nurturing connections, you'll set the stage for a productive and fulfilling year ahead.

February

February 2025 is a month of creativity, connection, and introspection for Pisces. With the Sun in Aquarius for most of the month, the energy supports innovative thinking, networking, and exploring new ideas. As the Sun transitions into Pisces later in February, the focus shifts to self-expression, emotional depth, and aligning with your inner purpose. This is a time to embrace your unique strengths and set meaningful intentions for the year ahead.

Work

February emphasizes collaboration and creativity in Pisces' professional life.

- **Opportunities:** The Aquarius energy supports brainstorming, teamwork, and tackling projects requiring fresh perspectives. Late in the month, Pisces energy inspires creativity and emotional intelligence, making it an excellent time to refine your vision or present ideas.
- **Challenges:** Avoid overthinking or procrastinating on decisions, especially when working on complex tasks.

Advice: Use Aquarius' dynamic energy to network and innovate, and Pisces' intuitive influence to align your actions with your long-term goals.

Finance

Your financial outlook in February highlights thoughtful planning and adaptability.

- **Opportunities:** Financial rewards may come from collaborations, creative ventures, or innovative problem-solving. This is a favorable time to reassess your budget and prioritize savings.
- **Challenges:** Avoid impulsive purchases, particularly during moments of social excitement or emotional highs.

Advice: Stick to a disciplined financial plan and focus on aligning your spending with your priorities. Seek advice if considering significant investments.

Love

February brings warmth and excitement to Pisces' love life, with Venus enhancing emotional connection and charm.

- **For Singles:** Romantic opportunities may arise through social events, shared activities, or intellectual pursuits. Aquarius energy fosters lighthearted connections, while Pisces later in the month deepens emotional intimacy.

- **For Those in Relationships:** Focus on open communication and shared experiences with your partner. Late February is ideal for planning special moments or having meaningful conversations.

Advice: Be open and authentic in your relationships. Use Aquarius energy to keep things exciting and Pisces energy to nurture emotional depth.

Health

Health-wise, February encourages Pisces to balance activity with self-care for overall well-being.

- **Strengths:** The Aquarius energy supports staying active and engaging in group activities or fitness routines. Pisces' influence later in the month promotes relaxation and emotional healing.
- **Challenges:** Stress from juggling responsibilities may affect your energy levels if not managed effectively.

Advice: Incorporate relaxation techniques like meditation or journaling into your routine. Focus on maintaining consistency in your wellness habits, and ensure you get enough rest to recharge.

Be Careful

- **Overcommitting:** Avoid taking on too many responsibilities, as this could lead to stress or burnout.
- **Impulsiveness:** Think carefully before making major decisions in financial or personal matters.
- **Neglecting Self-Care:** Balance your active schedule with downtime to maintain overall well-being.

Advice

1. **Explore and Innovate:** Use Aquarius' energy to embrace new ideas and expand your horizons.
2. **Reflect and Nurture:** Embrace Pisces' influence to align your goals with your values and deepen your relationships.
3. **Prioritize Balance:** Maintain harmony between productivity and relaxation to sustain your energy and focus.

Additional Tips

- **Lucky Days:** February 10, 18, and 26 — Ideal for decision-making, networking, or creative pursuits.
- **Lucky Color:** Light Blue — This color symbolizes clarity, inspiration, and emotional calm.

- **Affirmation for February:** *"I balance creativity with practicality, creating harmony and growth in my life."*

February 2025 is a month of connection and inspiration for Pisces. By focusing on meaningful relationships, creative pursuits, and self-care, you'll navigate this dynamic period with clarity and confidence.

March

March 2025 is a month of empowerment, self-expression, and transformation for Pisces. With the Sun in your sign for most of the month, you'll feel energized, inspired, and ready to take charge of your dreams. This is a time to prioritize your goals, embrace your creativity, and let your intuition guide you. As the Sun transitions into Aries later in March, the focus shifts toward action, ambition, and building momentum for the future.

Work

March emphasizes creativity and initiative in Pisces' professional life.

- **Opportunities:** Pisces Energy supports innovative ideas, collaborative projects, and refining your vision. Late in the month, Aries' influence inspires confidence and bold decision-making, making it a great time to pitch ideas or take on leadership roles.
- **Challenges:** Avoid letting self-doubt or emotional sensitivity hinder your progress. Stay focused on your strengths.

Advice: Use Pisces' intuitive energy to align your work with your values, and Aries' drive to take decisive action toward your goals.

Finance

Your financial outlook in March highlights stability and thoughtful planning.

- **Opportunities:** Financial gains may come from creative projects, side ventures, or bonuses. This is also a good time to revisit your budget and align spending with your priorities.
- **Challenges:** Avoid impulsive spending or risky financial decisions, particularly during moments of excitement or emotional highs.

Advice: Stick to a disciplined financial plan and consider seeking advice before making major financial commitments.

Love

March brings passion and depth to Pisces' love life, with Venus enhancing connection and emotional intimacy.

- **For Singles:** Romantic opportunities may arise through social events, creative activities, or mutual connections. Pisces energy encourages meaningful conversations and emotional compatibility.

- **For Those in Relationships:** Focus on strengthening trust and emotional intimacy with your partner. Late March is perfect for planning shared adventures or discussing future goals.

Advice: Be open and authentic in your interactions. Use Pisces' nurturing energy to deepen connections and Aries' confidence to express your desires.

Health

Health-wise, March encourages Pisces to focus on self-care and energy management.

- **Strengths:** Pisces energy supports practices like yoga, meditation, and journaling, which promote relaxation and mental clarity. Aries' influence later in the month boosts physical vitality and motivation for fitness routines.
- **Challenges:** Emotional stress or overworking may affect your energy levels if not managed properly.

Advice: Incorporate relaxation techniques into your routine. Prioritize a balanced diet, hydration, and adequate rest to maintain your well-being.

Be Careful

- **Overthinking:** Avoid letting self-doubt or emotional sensitivity slow you down. Trust your instincts and take action.
- **Neglecting Details:** While focusing on big-picture goals, ensure you're addressing finer details in your work and finances.
- **Burnout:** Balance your active lifestyle with adequate downtime to sustain your energy and focus.

Advice

1. **Prioritize Self-Expression:** Use Pisces' energy to embrace your creativity and let your unique voice shine.
2. **Act with Confidence:** As Aries season begins, step into leadership roles and pursue opportunities with determination.
3. **Maintain Balance:** Focus on self-care and meaningful relationships to create harmony in your life.

Additional Tips

- **Lucky Days:** March 8, 17, and 27 — Ideal for decision-making, creative pursuits, or strengthening relationships.

- **Lucky Color:** Coral Pink — This color symbolizes vitality, creativity, and emotional harmony.
- **Affirmation for March:** *"I embrace my creativity and act with confidence, creating harmony and success in my life."*

March 2025 is a month of inspiration and empowerment for Pisces. By focusing on meaningful goals, nurturing connections, and embracing your strengths, you'll navigate this transformative period with confidence and clarity.

April

April 2025 is a month of action, reflection, and meaningful progress for Pisces. With the Sun in Aries for most of the month, the energy emphasizes ambition, bold decision-making, and seizing new opportunities. As the Sun transitions into Taurus later in April, the focus shifts toward grounding, stability, and building a strong foundation for long-term goals. This blend of dynamic action and practical grounding makes April a highly productive and transformative time.

Work

April emphasizes initiative and strategic growth in Pisces' professional life.

- **Opportunities:** Aries Energy supports taking bold steps in your career, pursuing leadership roles, and embracing dynamic projects. Late in the month, Taurus' influence helps you solidify your efforts, making it an ideal time to focus on sustainability and long-term planning.
- **Challenges:** Balancing Aries' fast-paced energy with Taurus' slower, methodical approach may feel challenging. Avoid rushing decisions without proper evaluation.

Advice: Use Aries' confidence to take action on new opportunities and Taurus' practical energy to refine and stabilize your plans.

Finance

Your financial outlook in April highlights stability and growth.

- **Opportunities:** Financial gains may come from promotions, entrepreneurial ventures, or investments. Taurus Energy later in the month encourages thoughtful budgeting and aligning spending with your priorities.
- **Challenges:** Avoid impulsive purchases or risky investments during moments of excitement or urgency.

Advice: Focus on saving and making informed financial decisions. Seek professional advice for major investments.

Love

April brings passion and emotional stability to Pisces' love life.

- **For Singles:** Romantic opportunities may arise through work, social events, or shared hobbies. Aries energy inspires confidence and boldness in approaching potential partners, while Taurus later in the month encourages deeper emotional connections.

- **For Those in Relationships:** Focus on reigniting passion and celebrating your bond with your partner. Late April is perfect for creating stability and planning future goals together.

Advice: Be present and genuine in your interactions. Use Aries' adventurous energy to keep things exciting and Taurus' grounding influence to nurture trust and intimacy.

Health

Health-wise, April encourages Pisces to balance physical activity with relaxation for overall well-being.

- **Strengths:** Aries energy supports increased physical activity and motivation, making it a great time to boost your fitness routine. Taurus' influence later in the month promotes grounding practices like yoga or mindfulness for relaxation.
- **Challenges:** Overexertion or neglecting rest during Aries' busy energy may lead to fatigue if not managed properly.

Advice: Incorporate both dynamic exercise and calming practices into your routine. Focus on maintaining a balanced diet, staying hydrated, and ensuring you get enough sleep.

Be Careful

- **Impulsiveness:** Avoid making hasty decisions, particularly in financial or professional matters. Take time to evaluate your options.
- **Overworking:** Don't overload yourself with responsibilities, as this could lead to stress or burnout.
- **Neglecting Details:** Pay attention to finer points in your work or personal relationships, especially during the Taurus season.

Advice

1. **Take Bold Steps:** Use Aries' energy to pursue new opportunities with confidence and determination.
2. **Ground Your Efforts:** As Taurus season begins, focus on refining your plans and ensuring long-term stability.
3. **Nurture Connections:** Strengthen bonds with loved ones through meaningful gestures and open communication.

<u>*Additional Tips*</u>

- **Lucky Days:** April 9, 17, and 28 – Ideal for decision-making, creative projects, or strengthening relationships.
- **Lucky Color:** Emerald Green – This color symbolizes growth, grounding, and renewal.
- **Affirmation for April:** *"I take bold action and create stability, aligning my efforts with my purpose and dreams."*

April 2025 is a month of empowerment and grounding for Pisces. By focusing on ambitious goals, meaningful relationships, and balanced self-care, you'll navigate this dynamic and transformative period with clarity and confidence.

May

May 2025 is a month of stability, reflection, and meaningful progress for Pisces. With the Sun in Taurus for most of the month, the energy supports grounding, consistency, and building secure foundations in your personal and professional life. As the Sun transitions into Gemini later in May, the focus shifts toward adaptability, communication, and exploring new ideas. This combination of practicality and curiosity makes May a productive and enriching time for Pisces.

Work

May emphasizes focus and collaboration in Pisces' professional life.

- **Opportunities:** Taurus energy supports steady progress, completing ongoing tasks, and aligning your efforts with long-term goals. Late in the month, Gemini's influence inspires creativity and networking, making it an excellent time to explore dynamic projects or build connections.
- **Challenges:** Avoid becoming too fixed in your approach. Adapting to new perspectives will help you navigate opportunities effectively.

Advice: Use Taurus' energy to solidify your work and Gemini's dynamic influence to innovate and explore new possibilities.

Finance

Your financial outlook in May highlights stability and thoughtful planning.

- **Opportunities:** Financial gains may come from disciplined budgeting, successful investments, or collaborative ventures. This is also a favorable time to assess your savings and set new financial goals.
- **Challenges:** Avoid overspending on luxuries or indulging in impulse purchases, particularly during moments of excitement in the Gemini season.

Advice: Stick to a practical budget and focus on building financial security. Seek advice for significant financial decisions.

Love

May brings warmth and connection to Pisces' love life, with Venus enhancing harmony and emotional depth.

- **For Singles:** Romantic opportunities may arise through shared activities, social gatherings, or intellectual pursuits. Taurus energy encourages meaningful and stable connections, while Gemini later in the month brings playful and lighthearted interactions.

- **For Those in Relationships:** Focus on nurturing trust and emotional stability with your partner. Late May is ideal for planning fun outings or having deep, meaningful conversations about your shared future.

Advice: Be open and present in your relationships. Use Taurus energy to deepen bonds and Gemini energy to keep things fresh and exciting.

Health

Health-wise, May encourages Pisces to maintain balance and focus on consistency in wellness routines.

- **Strengths:** Taurus Energy supports grounding practices like yoga, meditation, or nature walks to promote relaxation and resilience. Late in the month, Gemini's influence inspires physical activity and social engagement to boost overall well-being.
- **Challenges:** Stress from overcommitting or neglecting self-care may affect your energy levels if not managed effectively.

Advice: Maintain a balanced diet, stay hydrated, and prioritize rest. Incorporate both relaxation and physical activity into your routine to sustain energy.

<u>*Be Careful*</u>

- **Overindulgence:** Avoid overspending or indulging in unhealthy habits, particularly during social events or celebrations.
- **Stubbornness:** While focusing on stability, remain open to new ideas and opportunities.
- **Impatience:** Balance your long-term goals with realistic timelines to avoid frustration.

<u>*Advice*</u>

1. **Build Stability:** Use Taurus energy to create secure foundations in your work, finances, and relationships.
2. **Stay Curious:** Embrace Gemini's influence to explore new opportunities, ideas, and connections.
3. **Prioritize Self-Care:** Balance your responsibilities with relaxation and meaningful interactions to maintain harmony.

<u>*Additional Tips*</u>

- **Lucky Days:** May 10, 18, and 29 — Ideal for decision-making, networking, or creative pursuits.
- **Lucky Color:** Light Yellow — This color symbolizes clarity, inspiration, and vitality.
- **Affirmation for May:** *"I create stability and embrace new possibilities, aligning my actions with my highest purpose."*

May 2025 is a month of grounding and exploration for Pisces. By focusing on thoughtful planning, meaningful relationships, and balanced self-care, you'll navigate this productive period with clarity and confidence.

June

June 2025 is a month of adaptability, exploration, and connection for Pisces. With the Sun in Gemini for most of the month, the energy supports communication, learning, and broadening your horizons. As the Sun transitions into Cancer later in June, the focus shifts to emotional depth, nurturing relationships, and creating balance between your ambitions and personal life. This mix of intellectual curiosity and heartfelt connection makes June an enriching and transformative time for Pisces.

Work

June emphasizes collaboration and dynamic thinking in Pisces' professional life.

- **Opportunities:** Gemini Energy supports networking, brainstorming, and innovative projects. Late in the month, Cancer's influence encourages a more nurturing approach, making it an excellent time to solidify workplace relationships and focus on long-term strategies.
- **Challenges:** Balancing Gemini's fast-paced energy with Cancer's emotional depth may feel challenging. Avoid procrastination or being overly scattered in your efforts.

Advice: Use Gemini's dynamic energy to explore new ideas and Cancer's intuitive influence to align your goals with your values.

Finance

Your financial outlook in June highlights adaptability and cautious growth.

- **Opportunities:** Financial rewards may come from intellectual pursuits, creative collaborations, or strategic planning. This is a good time to reassess your budget and realign your financial goals.
- **Challenges:** Avoid impulsive spending during moments of excitement or social indulgence.

Advice: Stick to a disciplined budget and focus on saving for long-term goals. Consider seeking advice before making major financial decisions.

Love

June brings warmth and connection to Pisces' love life, with Venus enhancing harmony and emotional intimacy.

- **For Singles:** Romantic opportunities may arise through social gatherings, intellectual pursuits, or shared hobbies. Gemini energy fosters lively and playful interactions, while Cancer's influence later in the month deepens emotional bonds.

- **For Those in Relationships:** Focus on nurturing trust and creating shared experiences with your partner. Late June is ideal for meaningful conversations and planning special moments together.

Advice: Be present and attentive in your relationships. Use Gemini's energy to keep things fun and Cancer's depth to strengthen your emotional connection.

Health

Health-wise, June encourages Pisces to balance physical activity with relaxation for overall well-being.

- **Strengths:** Gemini energy supports staying active and engaged in both mental and physical activities. Cancer's influence later in the month promotes emotional healing and self-care practices.
- **Challenges:** Stress from juggling responsibilities may affect your energy levels if not managed properly.

Advice: Incorporate mindfulness techniques like meditation or journaling into your routine. Focus on maintaining consistency in your fitness and nutrition, and prioritize rest to recharge.

Be Careful

- **Overcommitting:** Avoid taking on too many responsibilities or social engagements, as this could lead to stress or burnout.
- **Neglecting Details:** While focusing on broad goals, ensure you address finer points, especially in work and financial matters.
- **Emotional Sensitivity:** Practice mindfulness to manage emotions and avoid misunderstandings in relationships.

Advice

1. **Stay Open-Minded:** Use Gemini's influence to explore new opportunities and expand your horizons through learning and networking.
2. **Nurture Connections:** Embrace Cancer's energy to deepen relationships and prioritize meaningful interactions.
3. **Focus on Balance:** Maintain harmony by balancing your responsibilities with relaxation and self-care.

<u>***Additional Tips***</u>

- **Lucky Days:** June 9, 17, and 26 — Perfect for decision-making, networking, or creative pursuits.
- **Lucky Color:** Sky Blue — This color symbolizes clarity, inspiration, and calmness.
- **Affirmation for June:** *"I balance exploration with emotional connection, creating harmony and growth in all areas of my life."*

June 2025 is a month of connection and curiosity for Pisces. By focusing on meaningful relationships, creative pursuits, and self-care, you'll navigate this dynamic period with confidence and clarity.

July

July 2025 is a month of emotional depth, creativity, and personal growth for Pisces. With the Sun in Cancer for most of the month, the focus is on nurturing your inner self, building strong connections, and fostering emotional stability. As the Sun transitions into Leo later in July, the energy shifts toward self-expression, ambition, and embracing your creative potential. This blend of introspection and bold action makes July a powerful and transformative time for Pisces.

Work

July emphasizes emotional intelligence and creativity in Pisces' professional life.

- **Opportunities:** Cancer Energy supports strengthening workplace relationships and focusing on projects that align with your values. Late in the month, Leo's influence inspires confidence, creativity, and leadership, making it a great time to pitch ideas or step into a more visible role.
- **Challenges:** Balancing your emotions with professional demands may feel challenging. Avoid overthinking and stay focused on your strengths.

Advice: Use Cancer's reflective energy to build strong foundations and Leo's bold energy to showcase your unique talents.

Finance

Your financial outlook in July highlights thoughtful planning and potential growth.

- **Opportunities:** Financial gains may come from creative projects, collaborations, or rewards for past efforts. Late in the month, Leo Energy encourages exploring new income opportunities or investments.
- **Challenges:** Avoid impulsive spending, especially during moments of excitement or emotional highs.

Advice: Stick to a disciplined financial plan and focus on aligning your spending with your long-term priorities.

Love

July brings warmth and emotional depth to Pisces' love life.

- **For Singles:** Romantic opportunities may arise through creative activities, mutual friends, or introspective moments. Cancer's influence encourages meaningful connections, while Leo's energy later in the month adds excitement and charm to your interactions.

- **For Those in Relationships:** Focus on building trust, resolving any misunderstandings, and creating memorable experiences with your partner. Late July is ideal for reigniting passion and celebrating your bond.

Advice: Be open and present in your interactions. Use Cancer energy to deepen emotional bonds and Leo energy to keep things lively and engaging.

Health

Health-wise, July encourages Pisces to prioritize emotional well-being and maintain physical vitality.

- **Strengths:** Cancer energy supports self-care practices like journaling, meditation, or spending time in nature to nurture emotional health. Leo's influence later in the month boosts physical energy, making it a great time for outdoor activities or fitness routines.
- **Challenges:** Emotional stress or overexertion may affect your energy levels if not managed effectively.

Advice: Focus on maintaining a balanced diet, staying hydrated, and incorporating relaxation techniques into your daily routine. Prioritize rest to recharge.

Be Careful

- **Emotional Sensitivity:** Avoid letting strong emotions cloud your judgment in personal or professional matters.
- **Overcommitting:** Don't take on too many responsibilities, as this could lead to stress or burnout.
- **Impulsiveness:** Think carefully before making significant decisions, particularly in financial or personal matters.

Advice

1. **Focus on Emotional Growth:** Use Cancer's energy to nurture meaningful relationships and align with your inner self.
2. **Embrace Creativity:** As Leo season begins, take bold steps toward expressing your unique talents and ambitions.
3. **Balance is Key:** Maintain harmony by prioritizing both introspection and action to create a fulfilling and productive month.

Additional Tips

- **Lucky Days:** July 8, 17, and 27 – Ideal for decision-making, creative projects, or strengthening relationships.
- **Lucky Color:** Rose Gold – This color symbolizes warmth, vitality, and emotional balance.
- **Affirmation for July:** *"I nurture my inner self and express my creativity, creating harmony and success in my life."*

July 2025 is a month of emotional connection and creative inspiration for Pisces. By focusing on meaningful relationships, thoughtful planning, and self-care, you'll navigate this transformative period with confidence and clarity.

August

August 2025 is a month of ambition, creativity, and self-expression for Pisces. With the Sun in Leo for most of the month, the energy encourages you to take bold steps in showcasing your talents, pursuing creative projects, and stepping into leadership roles. As the Sun transitions into Virgo later in August, the focus shifts to organization, refining your goals, and prioritizing long-term stability. This combination of dynamic action and meticulous planning makes August a productive and inspiring time.

Work

August emphasizes creativity and precision in Pisces' professional life.

- **Opportunities:** Leo energy supports standing out in your career, pursuing new opportunities, and expressing your unique ideas. Late in the month, Virgo's influence helps you focus on the details, making it an excellent time to finalize projects or streamline your workflow.
- **Challenges:** Balancing Leo's bold energy with Virgo's need for perfection may feel challenging. Avoid overanalyzing or procrastinating.

Advice: Use Leo's confidence to present your ideas and Virgo's practical approach to ensure they're executed effectively.

Finance

Your financial outlook in August highlights growth and cautious planning.

- **Opportunities:** Financial gains may come from creative ventures, promotions, or leadership roles. Late in the month, Virgo Energy encourages thoughtful budgeting and aligning your finances with your long-term goals.
- **Challenges:** Avoid overspending on luxury items or indulging in impulsive purchases during moments of excitement.

Advice: Focus on saving and planning for the future. Seek professional advice before committing to significant financial decisions.

Love

August brings passion and connection to Pisces' love life.

- **For Singles:** Romantic opportunities may arise through creative activities, social gatherings, or professional connections. Leo energy enhances your charisma, making you particularly attractive. Late August is ideal for forming meaningful and grounded connections.

- **For Those in Relationships:** Focus on reigniting passion and celebrating your relationship with your partner. Late in the month, Virgo's influence supports meaningful conversations and strengthens your bond.

Advice: Be open and expressive in your relationships. Use Leo's energy to keep things exciting and Virgo's grounding influence to nurture emotional stability.

Health

Health-wise, August encourages Pisces to balance energy and maintain consistency in wellness routines.

- **Strengths:** Leo's energy inspires physical activity and motivation, making it a great time to enhance your fitness routine or try new activities. Virgo's influence later in the month promotes healthy habits and discipline.
- **Challenges:** Overexertion or neglecting rest during Leo's busy energy may lead to fatigue if not managed carefully.

Advice: Incorporate both dynamic exercise and calming practices like yoga or meditation into your routine.

Focus on a balanced diet and prioritize hydration to sustain your vitality.

Be Careful

- **Overconfidence:** Avoid taking unnecessary risks or making impulsive decisions in financial or professional matters.
- **Burnout:** Don't overcommit responsibilities or neglect downtime, as this could lead to stress.
- **Neglecting Details:** Balance your big-picture thinking with attention to finer points, especially as Virgo season begins.

Advice

1. **Showcase Your Talents:** Use Leo's energy to embrace your creativity, take bold steps, and stand out in your endeavors.
2. **Refine Your Goals:** As Virgo season begins, focus on aligning your actions with your long-term vision and ensuring they're practical.
3. **Maintain Balance:** Prioritize self-care and relaxation alongside your ambitions to sustain your energy and focus.

<u>***Additional Tips***</u>

- **Lucky Days:** August 9, 18, and 28 — Ideal for decision-making, creative projects, or building relationships.
- **Lucky Color:** Golden Yellow — This color symbolizes vitality, confidence, and success.
- **Affirmation for August:** *"I express my creativity and align my efforts with purpose, creating harmony and success in my life."*

August 2025 is a month of confidence and productivity for Pisces. By focusing on ambitious goals, meaningful connections, and disciplined planning, you'll make the most of this dynamic and fulfilling period.

September

September 2025 is a month of focus, refinement, and balance for Pisces. With the Sun in Virgo for most of the month, the energy supports organization, self-improvement, and aligning your goals with practical strategies. As the Sun transitions into Libra later in September, the focus shifts to harmony, collaboration, and fostering meaningful relationships. This combination of detail-oriented planning and social connection makes September a productive and fulfilling time for Pisces.

Work

September emphasizes precision and collaboration in Pisces' professional life.

- **Opportunities:** Virgo Energy supports tackling detailed projects, streamlining workflows, and refining your skills. Late in the month, Libra's influence encourages teamwork, networking, and exploring creative solutions.
- **Challenges:** Balancing Virgo's perfectionism with Libra's emphasis on relationships may feel challenging. Avoid becoming overly critical of yourself or others.

Advice: Use Virgo's energy to focus on the finer details of your work and Libra's charm to strengthen professional relationships and collaborations.

Finance

Your financial outlook in September highlights stability and careful planning.

- **Opportunities:** Financial rewards may come from disciplined budgeting, well-executed projects, or successful investments. Libra Energy later in the month encourages exploring partnerships or shared ventures.
- **Challenges:** Avoid overanalyzing financial decisions or being overly frugal during social opportunities.

Advice: Stick to a practical budget and focus on long-term financial goals. Ensure your decisions are balanced and thoughtful.

Love

September brings warmth and connection to Pisces' love life, with Venus enhancing emotional stability and harmony.

- **For Singles:** Romantic opportunities may arise through work, intellectual pursuits, or shared activities. Virgo energy encourages meaningful and grounded connections, while Libra adds charm and excitement later in the month.

- **For Those in Relationships:** Focus on building trust, resolving misunderstandings, and nurturing your bond with your partner. Late September is ideal for planning special moments or deepening your emotional connection.

Advice: Be genuine and present in your interactions. Use Virgo's grounding energy to nurture stability and Libra's charm to keep things lively and harmonious.

Health

Health-wise, September encourages Pisces to maintain consistency and balance in wellness routines.

- **Strengths:** Virgo Energy supports self-care practices like mindful eating, yoga, or meditation that enhance physical and mental well-being. Libra's influence later in the month promotes balance and relaxation.
- **Challenges:** Overworking or neglecting rest may affect your energy levels if not managed effectively.

Advice: Focus on a balanced diet, regular exercise, and incorporating mindfulness into your routine. Prioritize rest to recharge and sustain your energy.

Be Careful

- **Overthinking:** Avoid becoming overly critical or bogged down by perfectionism, especially in work or personal matters.
- **Impatience:** Balance your drive for progress with realistic timelines to avoid frustration.
- **Neglecting Self-Care:** Ensure you're dedicating time to both productivity and relaxation to maintain overall well-being.

Advice

1. **Focus on Refinement:** Use Virgo's energy to fine-tune your plans and align your efforts with your goals.
2. **Strengthen Connections:** Embrace Libra's influence to nurture relationships and collaborate effectively.
3. **Maintain Balance:** Prioritize self-care and mindfulness alongside your responsibilities to create harmony.

<u>*Additional Tips*</u>

- **Lucky Days:** September 8, 17, and 27 – Ideal for decision-making, networking, or creative pursuits.
- **Lucky Color:** Forest Green – This color symbolizes growth, balance, and renewal.
- **Affirmation for September:** *"I align my actions with my goals, creating harmony and success in all areas of my life."*

September 2025 is a month of thoughtful planning and meaningful progress for Pisces. By focusing on refining your goals, nurturing relationships, and maintaining balance, you'll navigate this productive period with confidence and clarity.

October

October 2025 is a month of transformation, harmony, and connection for Pisces. With the Sun in Libra for most of the month, the energy supports collaboration, balance, and building meaningful relationships. As the Sun transitions into Scorpio later in October, the focus shifts to introspection, emotional depth, and embracing personal transformation. This blend of social engagement and introspection makes October a powerful and inspiring time for Pisces.

Work

October emphasizes collaboration and strategic decision-making in Pisces' professional life.

- **Opportunities:** Libra Energy supports teamwork, negotiating partnerships, and finding creative solutions to challenges. Late in the month, Scorpio's influence helps you focus on complex tasks and long-term strategies.
- **Challenges:** Balancing Libra's need for harmony with Scorpio's intensity may feel challenging. Avoid overanalyzing situations or becoming overly cautious.

Advice: Use Libra's charm to strengthen professional relationships and Scorpio's determination to tackle meaningful projects.

Finance

Your financial outlook in October highlights balance and potential growth.

- **Opportunities:** Financial rewards may come from partnerships, creative ventures, or investments. This is also a favorable time to reassess your financial goals and align your spending with your priorities.
- **Challenges:** Avoid impulsive spending, particularly during moments of emotional highs or social indulgence.

Advice: Focus on financial discipline and long-term planning. Seek advice before making major financial commitments.

Love

October brings passion and depth to Pisces' love life, with Venus enhancing connection and emotional intimacy.

- **For Singles:** Romantic opportunities may arise through social gatherings, mutual interests, or introspective moments. Libra's influence encourages lighthearted and harmonious connections, while Scorpio's energy later in the month adds emotional depth and passion.

- **For Those in Relationships:** Focus on nurturing trust and deepening your bond with your partner. Late October is perfect for resolving conflicts and reigniting passion.

Advice: Be open and present in your relationships. Use Libra's energy to maintain harmony and Scorpio's influence to strengthen intimacy.

Health

Health-wise, October encourages Pisces to prioritize balance and emotional well-being.

- **Strengths:** Libra Energy supports engaging in group fitness activities, mindfulness practices, or social outings that promote relaxation and joy. Scorpio's influence later in the month inspires transformative wellness habits.
- **Challenges:** Stress from overcommitting or emotional intensity may affect your energy levels if not managed carefully.

Advice: Incorporate relaxation techniques and focus on maintaining consistency in your wellness routine. Balance activity with rest and self-care.

Be Careful

- **Overthinking:** Avoid overanalyzing personal or professional matters. Trust your instincts and take action when necessary.
- **Burnout:** Balance your active lifestyle with adequate downtime to avoid exhaustion.
- **Emotional Sensitivity:** Practice mindfulness to manage strong emotions and avoid miscommunication.

Advice

1. **Foster Relationships:** Use Libra's influence to nurture meaningful connections and work effectively in teams.
2. **Embrace Transformation:** As Scorpio season begins, focus on aligning your goals with your values and embracing change.
3. **Prioritize Self-Care:** Balance your ambitions with relaxation and mindfulness to maintain harmony and clarity.

- **Lucky Days:** October 9, 18, and 28 – Perfect for decision-making, creative pursuits, or strengthening relationships.
- **Lucky Color:** Deep Maroon – This color symbolizes resilience, transformation, and grounding.
- **Affirmation for October:** *"I balance connection with introspection, creating harmony and growth in all areas of my life."*

October 2025 is a month of dynamic energy and meaningful progress for Pisces. By focusing on relationships, personal growth, and self-care, you'll navigate this transformative period with confidence and clarity.

November

November 2025 is a month of introspection, transformation, and inspiration for Pisces. With the Sun in Scorpio for most of the month, the energy encourages deep reflection, emotional growth, and tackling personal challenges with resilience. As the Sun transitions into Sagittarius later in November, the focus shifts toward exploration, optimism, and expanding your horizons. This blend of emotional depth and adventurous energy makes November a powerful and fulfilling time for Pisces.

Work

November emphasizes focus and innovation in Pisces' professional life.

- **Opportunities:** Scorpio Energy supports diving into complex projects, refining long-term strategies, and addressing challenges with determination. Late in the month, Sagittarius' influence encourages creative problem-solving and exploring dynamic opportunities.
- **Challenges:** Balancing Scorpio's intensity with Sagittarius' spontaneous energy may feel challenging. Avoid rushing decisions without proper evaluation.

Advice: Use Scorpio's transformative energy to refine your plans and Sagittarius' optimistic influence to explore new paths with confidence.

Finance

Your financial outlook in November highlights planning and potential growth.

- **Opportunities:** Financial gains may come from past investments, bonuses, or exploring new income streams. Late in the month, Sagittarius energy inspires you to think expansively and consider new financial strategies.
- **Challenges:** Avoid impulsive financial decisions, particularly during moments of enthusiasm or emotional highs.

Advice: Stick to a disciplined budget and focus on aligning your financial decisions with your long-term priorities.

Love

November brings passion and connection to Pisces' love life.

- **For Singles:** Romantic opportunities may arise through introspective activities, shared interests, or social gatherings. Scorpio energy deepens emotional connections, while Sagittarius adds excitement and charm to your interactions later in the month.

- **For Those in Relationships:** Focus on resolving conflicts, building trust, and creating shared experiences with your partner. Late November is ideal for reigniting passion and exploring new adventures together.

Advice: Be authentic and attentive in your relationships. Use Scorpio energy to nurture emotional bonds and Sagittarius energy to keep things fresh and engaging.

Health

Health-wise, November encourages Pisces to focus on emotional resilience and physical vitality.

- **Strengths:** Scorpio Energy supports transformative wellness habits, such as detoxifying routines, meditation, or introspection. Sagittarius' influence later in the month inspires physical activity and outdoor adventures.
- **Challenges:** Stress from emotional intensity or overcommitting may affect your energy levels if not managed carefully.

Advice: Incorporate relaxation techniques into your daily routine. Maintain consistency in your fitness and nutrition, and prioritize rest to recharge.

Be Careful

- **Emotional Overload:** Avoid letting intense emotions cloud your judgment in personal or professional matters.
- **Overconfidence:** During Sagittarius season, take calculated risks rather than acting impulsively.
- **Neglecting Details:** Balance your focus on big-picture goals with attention to finer details, especially in financial and work-related matters.

Advice

1. **Reflect and Realign:** Use Scorpio's energy to assess your goals and align your actions with your deeper values.
2. **Embrace Optimism:** As Sagittarius season begins, step into your power with confidence and explore dynamic opportunities.
3. **Maintain Balance:** Prioritize self-care, meaningful connections, and thoughtful planning to sustain your energy and focus.

<u>***Additional Tips***</u>

- **Lucky Days:** November 8, 17, and 27 – Ideal for decision-making, networking, or creative pursuits.
- **Lucky Color:** Deep Purple – This color symbolizes transformation, intuition, and resilience.
- **Affirmation for November:** *"I embrace transformation and align my actions with my purpose, creating harmony and success in all areas of my life."*

November 2025 is a month of deep reflection and growth for Pisces. By focusing on meaningful connections, thoughtful planning, and self-care, you'll navigate this transformative period with clarity and confidence.

December

December 2025 is a month of optimism, exploration, and preparation for Pisces. With the Sun in Sagittarius for most of the month, the energy supports broadening your horizons, setting new goals, and embracing adventure. As the Sun transitions into Capricorn later in December, the focus shifts to discipline, organization, and laying the groundwork for long-term success. This blend of expansive thinking and practical action makes December a rewarding and productive time for Pisces as you prepare for the new year.

Work

December emphasizes creativity and strategic planning in Pisces' professional life.

- **Opportunities:** Sagittarius Energy supports brainstorming, networking, and exploring dynamic opportunities. Late in the month, Capricorn's influence encourages refining your plans, organizing priorities, and focusing on long-term career goals.
- **Challenges:** Balancing Sagittarius' spontaneity with Capricorn's structure may feel challenging.

Avoid rushing decisions without proper evaluation.

Advice: Use Sagittarius' energy to dream big and Capricorn's discipline to turn those dreams into actionable goals.

Finance

Your financial outlook in December highlights stability and growth.

- **Opportunities:** Financial rewards may come from year-end bonuses, successful investments, or creative projects. This is also a favorable time to review your budget and plan for upcoming expenses in 2026.
- **Challenges:** Avoid overspending on holiday-related expenses or indulgent purchases during moments of excitement.

Advice: Stick to a disciplined financial plan, prioritize savings, and focus on long-term financial security.

Love

December brings warmth and excitement to Pisces' love life.

- **For Singles:** Romantic opportunities may arise through social gatherings, travel, or intellectual pursuits. Sagittarius energy encourages playful and exciting connections, while Capricorn later in the month supports deeper emotional bonds.
- **For Those in Relationships:** Focus on celebrating your connection through shared experiences, thoughtful gestures, and meaningful conversations. Late December is ideal for discussing plans and strengthening commitment.

Advice: Be open and attentive in your relationships. Use Sagittarius' energy to keep things lively and Capricorn's grounding influence to nurture stability and trust.

Health

Health-wise, December encourages Pisces to maintain balance and focus on well-being.

- **Strengths:** Sagittarius energy supports physical activity, exploration, and trying new fitness routines. Capricorn's influence later in the month inspires consistency and discipline in maintaining healthy habits.
- **Challenges:** Overindulgence in food, drink, or social activities during the holiday season may affect your energy if not managed properly.

Advice: Practice moderation, maintain a balanced diet, and prioritize relaxation. Incorporate mindfulness and self-care into your routine to stay energized and focused.

Be Careful

- **Overspending:** Avoid exceeding your budget on gifts, travel, or holiday celebrations.
- **Burnout:** Balance social activities with rest to avoid overstretching yourself during this busy time.
- **Neglecting Details:** Pay attention to fine details, especially in work or financial planning, as Capricorn season begins.

Advice

1. **Celebrate and Reflect:** Use Sagittarius' energy to celebrate your achievements and reflect on your journey throughout the year.
2. **Set Goals:** Embrace Capricorn's influence to organize your priorities and set realistic goals for 2026.

Nurture Relationships: Strengthen bonds with loved ones by expressing gratitude and creating meaningful moments.

<u>*Additional Tips*</u>

- **Lucky Days:** December 6, 15, and 30 – Perfect for decision-making, creative pursuits, or building relationships.
- **Lucky Color:** Midnight Blue – This color symbolizes wisdom, clarity, and strength.
- **Affirmation for December:** *"I celebrate my journey and align my goals with purpose, creating harmony and success in my life."*

December 2025 is a month of celebration, preparation, and optimism for Pisces. By focusing on meaningful connections, disciplined planning, and self-care, you'll end the year on a high note and set the stage for a prosperous 2026

Good Luck For 2025